DOCUMENTS OF DEMOCRACY

The Mayflower Compact

By Sadie Silva

New York

Published in 2022 by Cavendish Square Publishing, LLC
29 E. 21st Street, New York, NY 10010

First Edition

Portions of this work were originally authored by Kristen Rajczak and published as *The Mayflower Compact* (*Documents That Shaped America*). All new material this edition authored by Sadie Silva.

Library of Congress Cataloging-in-Publication Data

Names: Silva, Sadie, author.
Title: The Mayflower Compact / Sadie Silva.
Description: First. | New York : Cavendish Square Publishing, [2022] | Series: The inside guide: documents of democracy | Includes bibliographic references and index.
Identifiers: LCCN 2020042882 | ISBN 9781502660367 (library binding) | ISBN 9781502660343 (paperback) | ISBN 9781502660350 (set) | ISBN 9781502660374 (ebook)
Subjects: LCSH: New Plymouth Colony. Mayflower Compact–Juvenile literature. | Mayflower (Ship)–Juvenile literature. | Pilgrims (New Plymouth Colony)–Juvenile literature. | Massachusetts–History–New Plymouth, 1620-1691–Juvenile literature.
Classification: LCC F68 .S583 2022 | DDC 974.4/02–dc23
LC record available at https://lccn.loc.gov/2020042882

Editor: Caitie McAneney
Copyeditor: Jill Keppeler
Designer: Jessica Nevins

The photographs in this book are used by permission and through the courtesy of: Cover File:The Mayflower Compact 1620 cph.3g07155.jpg/Wikimedia Commons; p. 4 API/Gamma-Rapho via Getty Images; pp. 6, 18 (top), 25, 29 (top) The Print Collector/Print Collector/Getty Images; pp. 7, 8, 18 (bottom), 23 Bettmann/Getty Images; p. 9 Hulton Archive/Getty Images; pp. 10, 27 (bottom) Courtesy of the National Archives; p. 12 Ann Ronan Pictures/Print Collector/Getty Images; p. 13 Three Lions/Hulton Archive/Getty Images; p. 14 duncan1890/DigitalVision Vectors/Getty Images; p. 15 MPI/Getty Images; p. 16 Herbert Orth/The LIFE Images Colleciton via Getty Images/Getty Images; p. 19 Rischgitz/Getty Images; p. 20 Ed Vebell/Getty Images; p. 21 PhotoQuest/Getty Images; p. 22 Charles Phelps Cushing/ClassicStock/Getty Images; p. 24 Archive Photos/Getty Images; p. 26 Kevin Fleming/Corbis/VCG/Corbis Documentary/Getty Images Plus/Getty Images; p. 27 (top) Universal History Archive/Getty Images; p. 29 (bottom) Morphart Creation/Shutterstock.com.

CPSIA compliance information: Batch #CW22CSQ: For further information contact Cavendish Square Publishing LLC, New York, New York, at 1-877-980-4450.

Printed in the United States of America

CONTENTS

In November 1620, despite deadly storms and rough seas, 102 men, women, and children landed in today's Massachusetts on a ship called the *Mayflower*.

LEAVING ENGLAND

The Mayflower Compact is known today as the first written framework of government established in today's United States. It was created by the Pilgrims in 1620 after a long voyage on the *Mayflower* from England to North America. The agreement was made before they even stepped foot on land. This 200-word document set the tone for **democracy** in America.

Escaping Persecution

Many of the people who traveled on the *Mayflower* were leaving England for the promise of religious freedom. Today, we call them Pilgrims, though that name wasn't widely used to describe them until the early 1800s. A pilgrim is usually anyone who takes a long journey, often for religious reasons.

Religion had become an issue in England after King Henry VIII turned

Fast Fact

The word "pilgrim" was used by William Bradford, who traveled on the *Mayflower*. He wrote, "They knew they were pilgrims, and looked not much on those things, but lifted up their eyes to the heavens, their dearest country; and quieted their spirits."

Henry VIII ruled England for 36 years and had 6 wives. He fought with the Catholic Church when he tried to end his first marriage.

against the Roman Catholic Church. He established a new church called the Church of England in 1534 and made himself its leader.

One group, called Puritans, wanted changes made to the church. Others, called Separatists, wanted to separate from the Church of England and form new churches. Some Separatist **congregations** wanted to find a new home where they could practice their religion in peace.

Finding a New Home

Some Separatists left England in 1608 and settled in Holland (the Netherlands). Though the Separatists stayed in the Dutch city of Leiden for more than 10 years, they weren't content there. They could practice their faith openly, but it was difficult to find good work and keep their English **heritage** alive. By 1620, some Separatists were ready to leave. They decided to go to the British colonies in

Fast Fact

During the 1600s, it was illegal in England to belong to any church other than the Church of England. **Dissenters** were fined and could even be thrown in jail.

North America, while others, including their minister John Robinson, stayed behind.

The Separatists turned to the Virginia Company for money and supplies. In exchange, the Separatists agreed to send natural resources such as wood and furs from the colonies to the company for seven years. Their land and homes would belong to the Virginia Company during that period too.

The Separatists planned to establish a farming community in the northern part of the Virginia Colony, near present-day New York City. The Virginia Company granted them a charter stating they had permission from the king for their settlement. They then made preparations to leave Holland for England—and after that, the New World.

In this image, Separatist minister John Robinson preaches to people as they leave Holland on the *Speedwell*. It would take them to England for their voyage to America.

THE VIRGINIA COMPANY

The Virginia Company of London was a group made up of investors that had been chartered by British King James I to establish a North American colony in 1606. This colony would give England a new source of natural resources and a new market for their goods. The Virginia Company founded the first permanent English settlement at Jamestown in 1607. People would pay the company for their voyage to the New World, and they'd pay to use the land once they got there. However, there were many challenges to setting up colonies an ocean away, from disease to fighting with Native peoples.

This was the seal of the Virginia Company.

People wave as the *Mayflower* leaves England. Some of the Separatists had to stay behind and wait until they could join their congregation in America.

All Together Now

Separatists departed for America on two boats—a larger one called the *Mayflower* and a smaller one called the *Speedwell*. When the two ships set out, the *Speedwell* started to leak. The ships had to turn back twice, delaying their departure. By September, the *Speedwell* was left behind, while the *Mayflower* set forth from Plymouth, England, to North America.

Some of the Pilgrims weren't Separatists. They were crew members and other passengers who also wished to travel to the New World. The Separatists sometimes called these passengers "strangers." The *Mayflower* had about 20 to 30 crewmembers, as well as officers and sailors. The passengers—both Separatists and "strangers"—made up the rest of the boat's **occupants**. Despite their differences, they had to complete this voyage together.

Fast Fact

Mayflower passengers had already been living on boats for a month and a half before their journey could even really begin. Some people gave up, while others packed onto the boat for the voyage.

Some of the Pilgrims relied on their deep faith to get them through the long sea voyage to set up their new colony.

A NEW WORLD

The voyage to America was not an easy one. The Pilgrims faced rough seas, seasickness, and unsanitary living conditions aboard the *Mayflower*. Their arrival in the New World—and the community and the rules for it they established—would change the course of American history.

The *Mayflower*

You might imagine the *Mayflower* as a passenger ship, since it carried 102 people. However, this was a cargo ship, built to transport goods. The *Mayflower* had much more cargo than expected, because it carried the cargo from the *Speedwell* too. The cargo was normally stored in the lower decks of the ship in an open storage area with low ceilings and no windows.

Fast Fact

One of the most famous people aboard the *Mayflower* was William Bradford. He helped write the Mayflower Compact, served as governor of the colony 31 times, and wrote *History of Plymouth Plantation, 1620–47*.

This painting shows the Pilgrims boarding the *Mayflower*, ready to set sail for America.

Fast Fact

A baby was born during the voyage. Passenger Elizabeth Hopkins gave birth to a son named Oceanus.

The crew lived on the more comfortable upper decks. The captain of the ship had large quarters, but passengers lived on the windowless lower deck where the *Mayflower* usually held its cargo. Packed together, without privacy or much room to move around, the *Mayflower* was a test of survival. The Pilgrims lived here for the 66-day journey across the Atlantic Ocean.

Crossing the Ocean

The Pilgrims set off from Plymouth, England, on September 6, 1620. Sailing across the ocean was much more dangerous in the 1600s than it is today. They had to be ready for storms and even pirates. Because the *Speedwell*'s leaks had delayed their departure, they were sailing the Atlantic during the stormy season. Part of the ship was damaged in a bad storm, but luckily it could be fixed. Seasickness was common, and other illnesses spread easily in the cramped living quarters.

The Pilgrims brought food such as bacon, biscuits, cabbage, and turnips—but they often felt too seasick to eat. Their vegetables ran out eventually, and they had to eat bowls of mush and oatmeal, which didn't have many nutrients. They were very weak by the time they landed. Surprisingly, only one person died on the voyage, though he was a sailor and not a Separatist.

The *Mayflower* encountered many storms on the Atlantic Ocean.

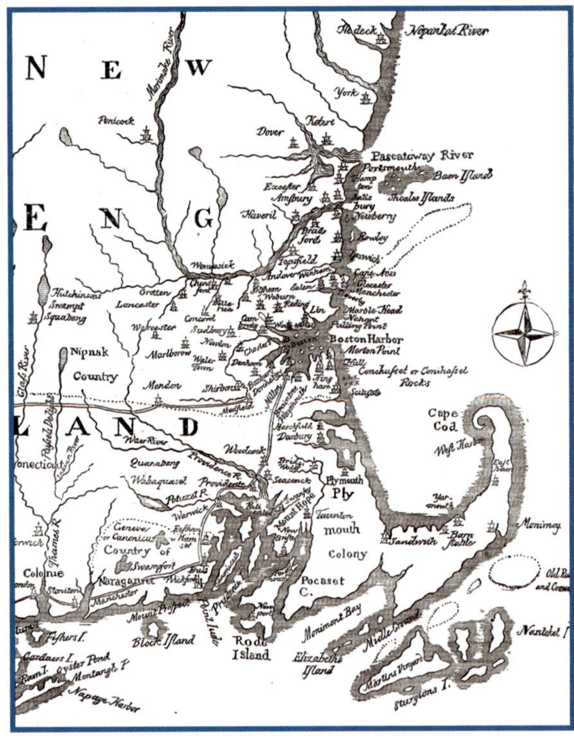

This 18th-century map of New England shows Cape Cod (to the east).

The Pilgrims' Arrival

After 66 days at sea, the *Mayflower* approached land. However, strong November winds had driven the ship much farther north than intended. Instead of traveling to the Hudson River, the *Mayflower* had sailed into Cape Cod, near what is now Provincetown Harbor. They tried to continue around Cape Cod and then south, but storms made this impossible. The group decided that it was too late in the year to keep going, and they chose to try to land in Cape Cod Bay.

However, the group now faced a turning point. The Virginia Company's charter applied only to an area of Virginia. When the group arrived in Cape Cod instead, the charter no longer legally bound them together. The Separatists and other passengers didn't have a shared faith keeping them together, either. Tensions began to build among them.

The Separatist leaders wanted a way to keep the passengers peacefully working together to survive. They needed to come to an agreement before they left the ship.

Fast Fact

Some of the Pilgrims thought they should break away and work for themselves instead of the Virginia Company, which added to tensions on the *Mayflower*.

EXISTING SETTLEMENTS

There were other English settlements in North America when the Pilgrims arrived, though they were farther south. Established in 1607, the settlement of Jamestown (in the Virginia Colony) was the first successful British settlement in North America. The colonists there had suffered deadly winters, diseases, and fights with Native peoples in their first years. However, by the time the Pilgrims left England, Jamestown was growing in population and prosperity. Tobacco crops were flourishing. The colonists had begun electing their own representatives to a colonial assembly headed by a royal governor. This success story was something the Pilgrims could strive for.

The Virginia Company made the first permanent English settlement in North America on the banks of the James River.

The forme was as followeth.

ame of god Amen. We whose names are underw
ll subiects of our dread soveraigne Lord K
race of god, of great Britaine, franc, & Irela
r of ye faith, &c.

undertaken, for ye glorie of god, and advan
stian faith and honour of our king & countrie, a v
first colonie in ye Northerne parts of Virgin
presents solemnly & mutualy in ye presence of
nother; covenant, & combine our selves togeathe
dy politick; for our better ordering, & preservatio
of ye ends aforesaid; and by vertue hearof to e
te, and frame shuch just & equall lawes, or
stitutions, & offices, from time to time, as shall
eete & convenient for ye generall good of ye Colon
e promise all due submission and obedience. I
we have hereunder subscribed our names a
·11· of November, in ye year of ye raigne of our
ing James of England, france, & Ireland
Scotland ye fiftie fourth. An: Dom. 1620.

s they chose, or rather
well approved among
nd after they had provided a place for their
store, (which were long in unlading for man

This is a copy of the Mayflower Compact. The original document has been lost to history.

MAKING THE MAYFLOWER COMPACT

The Mayflower Compact was necessary to unite those who arrived aboard the *Mayflower*. When they stepped off the ship, they would need to work together to build a settlement and protect one another from the challenges of the New World.

Crafting a Covenant

Until 1793, this document wasn't called the Mayflower Compact like it is today. Before then, it was sometimes called an "association and agreement" or a "solemn contract." It was even called a covenant, which is an agreement between people and an agreement between God and humans. This showed how Separatists used their religious beliefs to shape their founding document.

This covenant began with a **pledge** of loyalty and faith. First, the Mayflower Compact established that the signers were "Loyal Subjects" of King James. They promised that their voyage and the founding of

Fast Fact

The Mayflower Compact gave a broad description of how a government should oversee the group but not how it would be structured.

This image shows some of the signatures on the Mayflower Compact, including those of William Bradford and Myles Standish.

the colony "in the northern Parts of Virginia" had been undertaken for the "Advancement of the Christian Faith" and to honor their "King and Country."

The signers formally bound themselves together into a group they called the "civil Body Politick" for their "better Ordering and Preservation." It declared that the signers pledged to "enact, constitute, and frame such just and equal laws, **ordinances**, acts, constitutions, and offices ... for the general good of the colony." This reflected a promise of justice and equality within their governing body.

Fast Fact

The document was signed by 41 of the passengers. All of the signers were male, and they included most of the freemen, two servants, and three hired men.

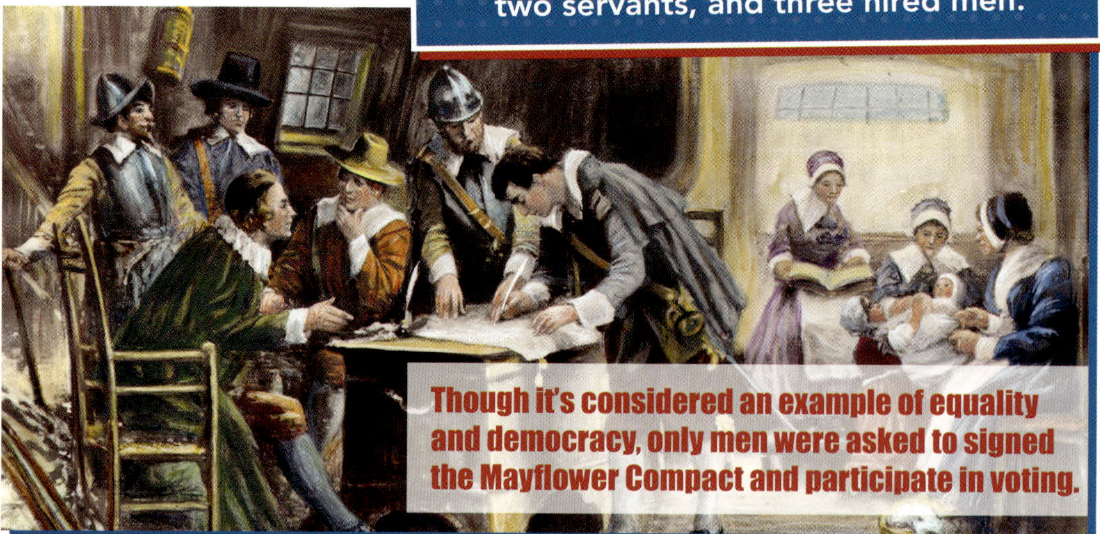

Though it's considered an example of equality and democracy, only men were asked to signed the Mayflower Compact and participate in voting.

SUBMISSION AND OBEDIENCE

The Separatists and other passengers often didn't get along. William Bradford wrote about noticing some people aboard who were "not well affected to unity … but gave some appearance of faction [separation]." Therefore, it would be beneficial to form an "association and agreement, that we should combine together in one body." By signing the Mayflower Compact together, they would pledge to stay together for the good of the colony. To suppress the **mutinous** ideas of some *Mayflower* passengers, the Mayflower Compact ended with a promise that the signers would give "all due Submission and Obedience," signaling an agreement to work together.

This artwork depicts the signing of the Mayflower Compact aboard the famed ship. The document was meant to unite the Pilgrims.

Myles Standish, depicted here in armor, was the military leader of Plymouth Colony. Standish helped explore the land, choose a site for settlement, and handle relations with Native peoples, which weren't always good.

Self-Governance

The colonists had to ask for another charter from England to have any right to the land they'd settled. However, upon its signing, the Mayflower Compact did set up the framework for a working government. This marked the first occurrence of European self-governance in the English colonies.

The Pilgrims chose John Carver as their governor, though he served for only a year before his death. William Bradford was then elected 31 times as governor, helping to set up a government in which some people had a voice through town meetings. He believed in private agriculture and religious **tolerance**.

Making a Home

Now that the Pilgrims had an agreement, they had to find a place to settle. They waited a few more weeks before leaving the *Mayflower*. They sent a group to find a suitable place for their

Fast Fact

Though elections weren't outlined in the document, the ideas behind the Mayflower Compact made this democratic exercise possible.

colony. The Pilgrim explorers chose the site of an abandoned Wampanoag settlement. Most of the tribe had died because Europeans had brought deadly illnesses several years before.

The site was ideal for the Pilgrims' needs. There was water, and there were cleared fields ready for planting. Plus, it was on a hill, which would help them spot anyone who approached. The Pilgrims called the place Plimoth (now Plymouth). The Pilgrims sailed into Plymouth Harbor in December 1620, ready to make a new community there. Today, people visit Plymouth Rock, a boulder which is said to be the stepping-stone that *Mayflower* passengers used to enter the New World.

This image shows the Pilgrims leaving the *Mayflower* after months at sea.

The Pilgrims left the *Mayflower* weak and weary from lack of proper nutrition and the wet, cramped conditions of the ship.

DEVELOPING DEMOCRACY

The Pilgrims didn't have an easy time building their colony. Many of the people who arrived on the *Mayflower* didn't survive very long. However, they used democratic principles even as their colony grew and changed throughout the years.

A Rough Beginning

Arriving in North America in the springtime would have given the Pilgrims the best chance of survival. They could have had a whole summer to make their settlement and get ready for winter. However, the Pilgrims arrived in November, just as winter was about to begin, and they had no time to prepare.

The first winter in Plymouth was cold and difficult. The Pilgrims continued to live on the ship while houses and other buildings were constructed on land. Many Pilgrims fell ill, and about half died during the winter of 1620 to 1621.

The *Mayflower* left the new Plymouth Colony for its return to England on April 5, 1621.

NATIVE LAND

Although England claimed large areas of land in North America, Native peoples had lived there for thousands of years. They had their own **cultures**, languages, and farming practices. The Pilgrims met a Native man called Squanto, who had been a captive in England and spoke their language. He helped the Pilgrims communicate with the Native peoples. In 1621, the Pokanoket tribe shared a feast with the Pilgrims in what is now known as the first Thanksgiving. Native people taught the Pilgrims about new crops. Later, colonists would **decimate** Native peoples through violence and disease.

This image shows Pilgrims meeting Samoset, the first Native American to call out to them in English when they arrived. Samoset introduced them to Squanto, who spoke English well.

This image shows Pilgrims approaching Massasoit, who was the chief of the Pokanoket tribe and leader of the Wampanoag Confederacy.

They suffered from diseases caused by cold weather, unsanitary conditions, and a lack of nutrients.

The weary Pilgrims began living in Plymouth in March 1621. The *Mayflower* returned to England the following month. With the help of Native peoples, the Pilgrims learned to prosper on the land.

Growing in Number

Plymouth Colony faced many challenges, but it became self-sustaining within 5 years. Soon, more Separatists who had been left in England made the voyage to Plymouth. By the 1640s, about 3,000 people lived in the colony. Colonists used the Mayflower Compact as the foundation of their government, which was mostly controlled by Separatists.

In 1630, about 1,000 Puritans sailed from England. Puritanism aimed to **purify** the Church of England of some leftover Catholic practices. They wanted to mold their colony to their strict religious beliefs. They settled the Massachusetts Bay Colony, including the cities of Salem and Boston.

In 1691, the Massachusetts Bay Colony was granted a new charter from England. It joined the Plymouth Colony to Massachusetts Bay under the British government. This charter replaced the Mayflower Compact.

Fast Fact

The Puritan's charter allowed them to set up a government in the colonies. It was a move toward democracy, though those who weren't part of their church couldn't vote.

As more people came to live in Plymouth in the 1630s, small towns formed around the main settlement. People began to choose representatives to speak for them at colonial government meetings.

Community and Equality

The Mayflower Compact left a lot unsaid, which has opened it up to **interpretation**. Some historians interpret the Mayflower Compact to mean that the Pilgrims wanted to create a government based on equality—but that's not stated in the document itself. Also, Plymouth was generally ruled by a small group of **elite** settlers. In addition, it's been said that the Pilgrims' writing of the Mayflower Compact implies a belief in government created by the people. This may be true, as all adult men could vote in elections, and later, the colonists chose representatives.

Fast Fact

We don't have the original Mayflower Compact. However, in 1622, a pamphlet called "Mourt's Relation" printed its text. This short document has been debated for many years.

President John Quincy Adams saw the Mayflower Compact as an important American document.

Again, though, this isn't directly stated in the Mayflower Compact.

Many agree the Pilgrims were ahead of their time when they established their government under the Mayflower Compact. Some people even think it influenced the Declaration of Independence and U.S. Constitution. This covenant saw the Pilgrims through challenges and prosperity and sowed the seeds of democracy in the New World.

Fast Fact

President John Quincy Adams once said the Mayflower Compact was the first modern example of a group of men acting as equals and agreeing to create a community and government.

The Declaration of Independence was another major document of democracy. In 1776, it declared a new and independent government for the people by the people.

MAYFLOWER COMPACT TIMELINE

1534 King Henry VIII of England leaves the Catholic Church and establishes the Church of England.

1552 Attending religious services outside the Church of England is considered unlawful with the passing of the Act of Uniformity.

1608 A Separatist congregation led by minister John Robinson and church elder William Brewster moves to Holland to practice its religion freely.

1616 A Wampanoag tribe in the Plymouth area is wiped out by disease.

July 1620 Separatists leave Leiden, Netherlands, for England.

August 5, 1620 The *Mayflower* and *Speedwell* depart for the New World. They turn back about a week later because of the *Speedwell*'s leaks.

August 23, 1620 The *Mayflower* and *Speedwell* depart again but turn back because of the *Speedwell*'s leaks.

September 6, 1620 The *Mayflower* leaves the *Speedwell* behind and departs for the Virginia Colony.

November 11, 1620 The *Mayflower* stops in Provincetown Harbor. The Mayflower Compact is signed.

December 20, 1620 The Pilgrims start to make their home in the abandoned Wampanoag village.

March 1621 Governor Carver, leader of Plymouth, and Massasoit, leader of the Wampanoag, sign a peace treaty.

April 1621 William Bradford becomes governor, a post he keeps for 30 years.

September/October 1621 The colonists and Native peoples come together for a harvest celebration.

THINK ABOUT IT!

1. Why do you think it was so important for Separatists to move to the New World?
2. Why might there have been tension between the Separatists and "strangers" on the ship?

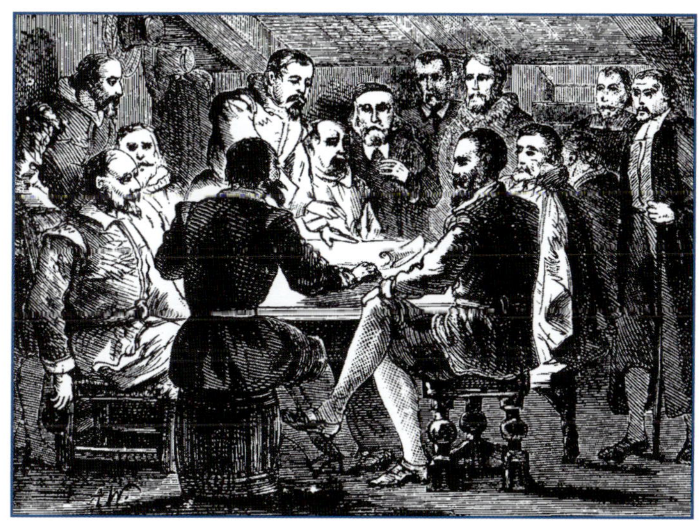

3. What are some benefits of the Pilgrims uniting upon arriving in the New World?
4. How do you think ideas from the Mayflower Compact have affected other documents of democracy in the United States?

GLOSSARY

congregation: A religious community.

culture: The beliefs and ways of life of a certain group of people.

decimate: To reduce a population greatly in number.

democracy: The free and equal right of every person to participate in a government.

dissenter: One who differs in opinion.

elite: The people in a society who are thought to be the greatest.

heritage: The traditions and beliefs that are part of the history of a group or nation.

interpretation: An explanation of the meaning of something.

mutinous: Describing people who rise against or refuse to obey or observe authority.

occupant: Someone who lives or stays in a place.

ordinance: A law or rule.

pledge: A binding promise or agreement to do something.

purify: To make something pure by removing unwanted qualities.

tolerance: Accepting other ideas, beliefs, or points of view.

FIND OUT MORE

Books

Jenner, Caryn. *Sailing on the Mayflower.* New York, NY: Kingfisher Books, 2019.

Miller, Marilyn, Ellen Scordato, and Dan Tucker. *Words that Built a Nation: Voices of Democracy That Have Shaped America's History.* New York, NY: Rodale Kids, 2018.

Streissguth, Thomas. *The Mayflower Story.* Minneapolis, MN: Abdo Publishing, 2018.

Websites

The Mayflower Compact
socialstudiesforkids.com/articles/ushistory/mayflowercompact.htm
Read the full Mayflower Compact and browse the names of the people who signed it.

The Pilgrims and Plymouth Colony
www.ducksters.com/history/colonial_america/pilgrims_plymouth_colony.php
Explore more history behind the Pilgrims' journey and first years in Plymouth Colony.

The Pilgrims: Mayflower Compact
ny.pbslearningmedia.org/resource/americanexperience27p-soc-compact/wgbh-americanexperience-the-pilgrims-mayflower-compact/
Watch this video from PBS about the Pilgrims and their defining document.

Publisher's note to educators and parents: Our editors have carefully reviewed these websites to ensure that they are suitable for students. Many websites change frequently, however, and we cannot guarantee that a site's future contents will continue to meet our high standards of quality and educational value. Be advised that students should be closely supervised whenever they access the Internet.

INDEX